Daisy Dirt

Written and illustrated by Zoe Carter

Photography by Andrea Peterson

Copyright Zoe Carter 2015

For Sheetal

Once upon a time there was a piece of dirt.

Sticky.
Smelly.
Worthless.

Her name was Daisy.

She tried so hard to be beautiful. She put a bow in her hair.

But it was no good.

Everyone who saw her wiped her away in disgust.

Penelope was a refined lady who loved to wear pearls and high-heeled shoes.

Much to her dismay, she stepped on Daisy.

'Help me, Walter!',
she shrieked to her
husband.

'I have a great glob of dirt
stuck to my beloved shoe.
Whatever am I to do?'

'There's no need to be so dramatic', Walter sighed.

'All you need to do is give your beloved shoe a wash in the sink.

Here, let me help you.'

Daisy spluttered under the tap and slid into a whirlpool of water.

Round and round she went, then down through the plughole.

She sloshed down the pipes and underground into the dirtiest place on earth, the sewer. The rats hated her.

Her eyes filled with tears. Even here, amongst filth and grime, she did not have a home. She did not belong.

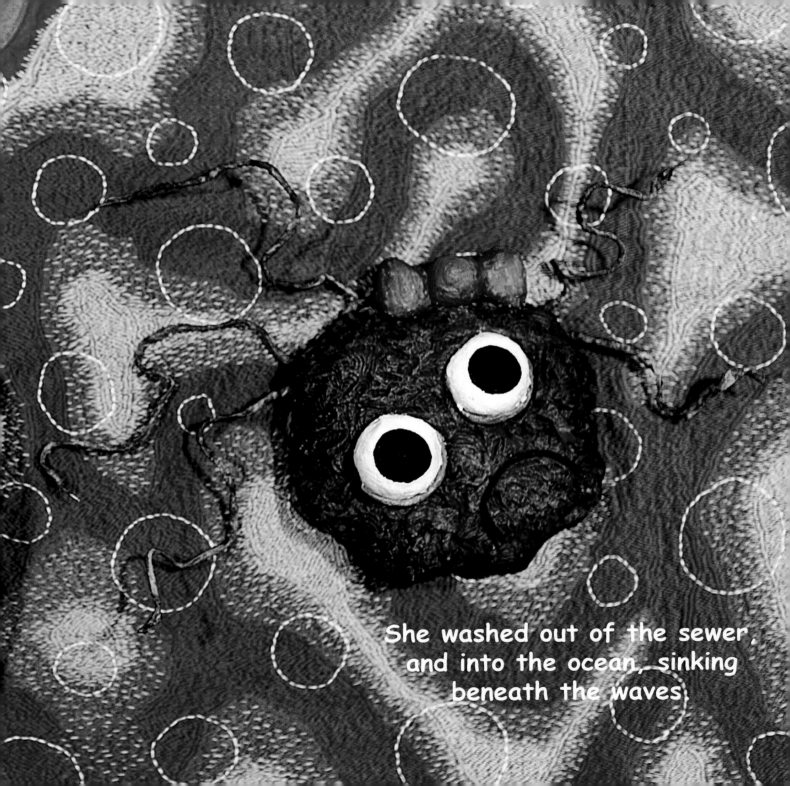

She washed out of the sewer, and into the ocean, sinking beneath the waves.

The sea creatures backed
away in horror.

She was too sad to care.

She floated through the
water, aimless and alone.

But she was not alone.
Oliver Oyster was waiting for her.

Her eyes widened with fear as he
opened his mouth and swallowed her up.

But this was not the end of her life.
This was the beginning.

For the first time she felt love.

A love that ran all over her and washed away her dirt and her hurt like the rain.

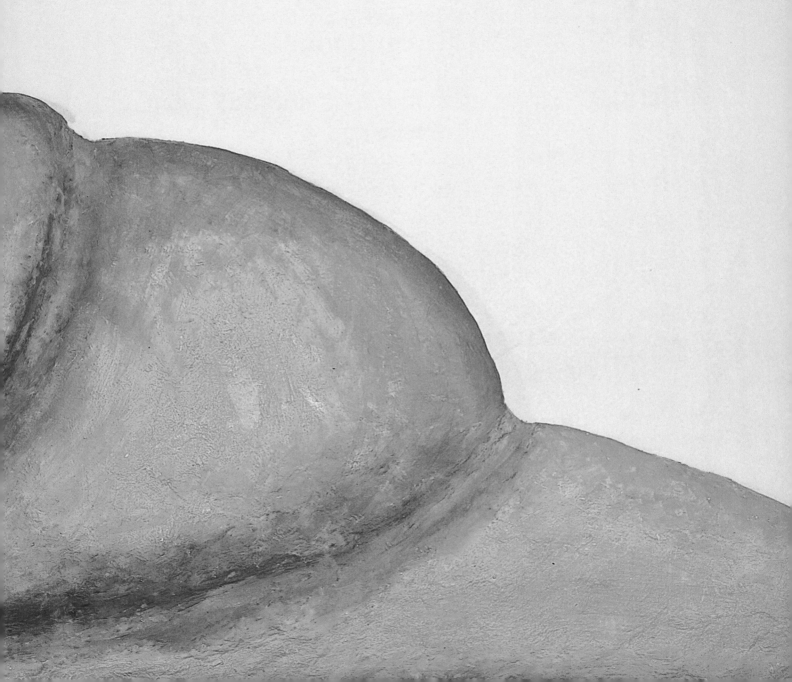

She closed her eyes and fell into a deep and blissful sleep.

'Wake up, Daisy.'
Oliver's voice jolted her out of sleep.
She had no idea how long she had been
dreaming.

'It's time to go outside.'

'Outside?', Daisy gasped
in horror.

'Don't make me go back outside.
They hate me out there. I am just a
worthless piece of dirt.'

'Oh Daisy', Oliver said tenderly. 'Look.'

He switched on the light.

Daisy could not believe her eyes. She looked in the mirror and saw a beautiful jewel.

'Who is that?', she asked in wonder.
'It's you', laughed Oliver.

'How did you do that?' she exclaimed.

'I have covered you with layer upon layer of pearl. You are precious through and through.'

Daisy saw that his skin that had once been pale and soft was bruised and scratched.

'Did I hurt you, Oliver?'
'Yes', he whispered, 'very badly.'
'Then why did you swallow me?', she asked through her tears.

'I did it for you, Daisy. To turn all of your dirt and all of your hurt into value and beauty. And now I want the whole world to see you.'

Suddenly, a hand reached beneath the water and grasped hold of Oliver.

Who could this be?

It was the King going for his early
morning swim.

His eyes shone with delight as he prised open
Oliver and found Daisy inside.

He swam back to the palace as fast as he could, and presented Daisy to his Queen.

The Queen loved Daisy. She wore her on a chain round her neck, so that Daisy would sit next to her heart.

'Anyone who belongs to Christ has become a new person. The old life is gone, a new life has begun!'
2 Corinthians 5:17 (NLT)

We are not alone in the universe.
God is watching us. He loves us with an everlasting love.

The world is broken.
God came to fix it.

If we put our trust in Jesus, he washes away every bad thing we have ever done or said or even thought.

We become what we were always meant to be: God's precious jewel.